Business Plan 101

A guide to combine the technical, financial, operational and marketing data will not only get you funded but will help you operate your business successfully.

By Juan Gallegos

Table of Contents

1. INTRODUCTION

So, you want to write a business plan? You've Googled pages of articles, looked at books on Amazon, read reviews on software – and you're still confused. The technical aspects seem overwhelming, and you're having trouble articulating your vision. What you need is a guide to combine the technical, financial, operational and marketing data that will not only get you funded but will help you operate your business successfully.

We will discuss how to write a business plan that includes a professional perspective on what the elements of a good business plans are, as well as how to make it both financially relevant as well as operationally viable. When we're done, you'll be able to communicate your actions and goals in a way that makes you confident that you're ready for this risk. A good business plan – a proper business plan – is both a guide for how you will spend the money to make money, and a promise to investors that you will do what you say to pay them back. Let's get started!

Most of what makes writing a business plan overwhelming is figuring out what you want to say, and how to say it. Before you try to write a plan in an investor-friendly format, first do some general writing that helps you articulate your plan to yourself. Take a deep breath and give yourself a break! The more you pressure yourself, the more difficult it will be to write something intelligent and reasonable.

Start by thinking about the answers to the questions below (or in the software, or in the book) and then write the answers down. You don't need to make it eloquent, or even in full sentences. You do need to answer key questions. Put yourself in the financier's shoes – if you were lending the same amount of money to someone you didn't know, what *answers* would need to hear to make you believe you would get your money back? Most financiers know what it takes to make money. They are looking to see if you do.

The first thing you need to do to be successful in your own business is this: Know your resources and do your homework. Not only will this impress your financier, it will give you the peace of mind that you truly are as prepared as possible to take one of the biggest risks of your life.

The Ugly Statistics

Now, let's move on to the bad news and get some things out of the way. According to Fundera.com:

"20% of small businesses fail in their first year, 30% of small businesses fail in their second year, and 50% of small businesses fail after five years in business. Finally, 70% of small business owners fail in their 10th year in business."[i]

This means that only 3 in 10 startups will still be around in 10 years. It's a sobering statistic.

Fortune.com cites a poll of failed start-up founders and found that the top 7 reasons for failure include:
> 42% - No Market Need
> 29% - Ran out of cash
> 23% - Not the right team
> 19% - Got outcompeted
> 18% - Pricing/Cost Issues
> 17% - Poor Product
> 17% - Need/Lack Business Model[ii]

The reason behind these failures is usually because most businesses fail to plan for the harsh and unexpected realities of *running* a business.

Before you create your business plan, you need to factor these considerations into your worst-case scenarios.

The cold reality of starting and operating your own business is that most businesses expect to be profitable too soon. There are unexpected operating costs that weren't anticipated because the business owners either didn't know the industry or business well enough or didn't do their homework because it seemed like they couldn't fail. Your attitude towards how you plan for your business is a key factor in whether you will be around in 10 years.

The good news is, you can create a business plan that gives you the best possible chance of success. The Fundera article also states that more small businesses are opening than closing, and that they are still 99.9% of the U.S. economy.

So, what will change the odds for you? Let's look at this from an investor or lender perspective for a moment. They are about to lend money to a business that has a 3 in 10 chance of succeeding and paying them back. How do they decide who gets their money?

What Financiers Look For

How much time you put into researching and communicating what it will take to operate the business and make it turn a profit will show in your business plan. Financiers read a lot of business plans. They've seen good one's failed and mediocre one's work. That means they have a keen understanding of what elements really makes a business work, what preparedness looks like, and who can pay back their investment. Charts and graphs make numbers easier to understand, but they don't take the place of a solid understanding of which activities and goals truly make a venture viable.

There are 3 things an investor or lender looks for in a business plan and proposal.
1. Owners expertise related to the new business

2. Credit history and score of the business/owner
3. Recoverability of the funds loaned or invested

Owner's Expertise

This encompasses several numbers of factors including the history of the business, the management team, and other relevant skills for running the specific business.

If your business is still a concept, then the history of the business is the history of your career and how that relates to the venture.
If you've been doing it as a hobby for a while, you'll need to discuss how well it's doing and how you're going to scale it up.
If you have an existing business that needs capital, you need to show how you create and capture revenue, and why growth is sustainable.

It's important to note here, that while having "passion" is tossed around as the intangible thing that makes a business fail or succeed, the truth is that passion isn't always sustainable when trouble hits. Financiers are looking for members of the management team who show commitment to a project over time, who have overcome hurdles in other businesses or jobs, and who have an in-depth understanding of the business and industry they are going to be competing in.

Expertise is also balanced against personal track records. Maybe you've had a career in a different industry, but you're trying to turn a long-term hobby into a full-time operation. This means that your career education and achievements show that you know how to become an expert is a different field, and a long-term hobby shows you are applying those same skills to the business. You'll need to explain how your skills, education and achievements have prepared you to take this new risk.

On the other hand, if you were an employee at a company in the same field, and have decided to open up a business that has little competition in a new location, or you're filling a niche in the industry that your current employer doesn't, then you can explain how you have a specific and related understanding of the field that has prepared you for this new venture.

At the very least, you should be a member of an industry organization where you can network, learn the best practices of other businesses like yours, recruit talent, and stay ahead of good and bad trends. Most investors know that an isolated business owner is more likely to fail faster than someone who knows where to find help and resources.

Owner's Credit History and Score

What does your credit say about you or your business? While the actual score is important, what's more important is why the score is what it is.

Is this a new business for you? Your credit should show that you pay your bills on time and aren't personally overextended. If possible, you should have some of your own money to put in as seed financing or have the records to show that you already have. Having skin in the game is important – lenders don't like it when only their money is at risk.

Is this a long-term hobby? If you've had cash flow for a while, you should be able to show that you've managed it well, upgraded your resources logically and know how to manage your expenses. Your credit history and score should reflect trustworthiness with money.

Is this an existing business? In this case the business should have a credit history that reflects proper use of credit, good standing with vendors, logical upgrades and recoupment of capital investments. Don't be surprised if your financier asks for letters of good standing from your vendors. How you handle your cash and disburse your profits should be explained as well.

Business credit scores differ a bit from personal credit scores. Depending on whether you're rated with Dun & Bradstreet, Equifax or

Experian, you'll find there's a mix of consideration for your business. Business.com lists the factors considered as follows:

- Number of years in business; more than two establishes viability.
- Annual business revenue.
- Business collateral.
- Recent lines of credit you have applied for and opened.
- Payment history.
- Percentage of available credit used - are you at your limit?[iii]

Perhaps your credit score is lower because you're currently using the most of your credit limits. If you've had to use your credit in order to keep up with growth, that's okay. You'll need to explain how the influx of cash will help you maintain great customer service and vendor relationships, and how you'll manage growth, so you don't get into the same predicament with the new investment funds. Be prepared to show documentation that supports the story of growth so far.

Quick tip: Investors are looking for controlled growth, not runaway growth. Runaway growth means that people and resources are overworked, and cash is strained trying to maintain sales. This usually leads to a decline in productivity, product quality, customer service and employee satisfaction. It also tends to exhaust the business owner, which leads to mistakes and poor judgment. If your investor suspects you don't know how to manage growth, they'll walk way. But if you have a plan for controlled growth that allows for recoupment of funds before the next growth cycle, they'll be much more interested in taking the risk with you because it means you know how to make money without taking unnecessary risks.

Recoverability of Funds

Financiers aren't interested in how much money you think you'll make. Their interested in how likely you are to pay them back with interest.

This means understanding the difference between revenue, cash flow, and profits.

Understand up front the difference between an investor and a lender. Lenders – usually banks – don't take risks. They need to know you can pay back the loan and want to think of you as a good investment. Investors do take risks – they want to think of you as a good risk. Depending on if you want a lender or an investor will determine how you discuss money repayment in your plan.

Revenue is the total income your business has earned and may include invoices or royalties not yet collected and in the bank. Revenue tells the picture of how much money is coming in. DryRun.com describes Revenue this way:

"The term 'revenue' is commonly used in business in other situations. For instance, you may say that you've earned more revenue from the sales of a specific product vs. another. You may also ask what revenue was earned for a particular contract or from a specific customer. In these cases, revenue refers to the income or earnings in each situation but may not refer to a timeframe. 'Revenue' never accounts for expenses and costs. It simply describes total money earned by the business."[iv]

Cash flow is the amount of cash or payments that come into the business as well as the expenses that go out. Cash flow tells the picture of how money moves through your business.

Profit is your expected Revenue minus your expenses. It can also be broken into two categories:

Gross Profit = Revenue minus your COGS (cost of goods sold)

Net Profit = Gross Profit minus all expenses

Your investors want to know if you understand the difference, and if you understand how these differences affect your business.

If you are an invoice or royalty driven business, money you are owed may not show up in time to pay bills that are due. That's the difference between Revenue and Cash Flow.

If you have heavy cash flow, but also have heavy expenses and find you don't have enough money left over for payroll, that's the difference between Cash Flow and Profit.

If you have only enough cash to pay your bills, taxes and employees, but there's not much leftover afterwards, that's the difference between Gross Profit and Net Profit.

Cash Flow pays a lender back on his loan. Net Profit pays back an investor for his risk. You'll need to know the difference depending on what type of financing you're looking for.

Quick Tip: Most small business owners don't take a salary. They take cash from the register or write a check to pay their personal bills haphazardly throughout the month. Don't make this mistake. Create a realistic salary for yourself that at least matches your lowest paid employee. This way, your net profit is a real profit *on top of* your salary. That's why you're starting a business, isn't it?

Financiers want to know that they will be paid back. They also want to know it's going to be worth it for you to keep running the business. You need to show you can pay your debts as well as reap the rewards of your efforts. A happy business owner is a motivated business owner – and a better risk to a lender.

Understanding how your lender or investor thinks is crucial to understanding what answers they need to their question, "how will I get my money back?" While this information isn't usually presented in a direct way, your understanding of it will help you write your plan in a way that tells your potential investor that you know what they want and you're going to give it to them. Be able to communicate this also creates a better foundation for a successful relationship with your investor.

2. WRITING THE PLAN

Choosing the format for your business plan takes a little research and is often subjective. You may prefer a software package that asks questions you need to answer. You might find an outline from a book you like or a template you found online.

Organizations like the SBA, Business.org, Business.com, Entrepreneur Magazine, Inc., PC Magazine and Bloomberg Businessweek all have blogs and articles rating software that show you what's available by price, type and usability. There is no one plan software that is best except that it's best for what you need.

- How specific are the questions and prompts?
- Does it have resources you can use to help understand what needs to be included in each section?
- Does it include financial plan templates or worksheets?
- Does it look professional?

These are only a few of the questions you need to consider.

Executive Summary

Your executive summary tells the investor what will be covered in the plan. Along with a brief description of the business, you should discuss the problem your business solves or niche that it serves, an overview of your target market and the highlights of your financials.

While the Executive Summary is the first thing an investor reads, you should write it last. This is a preview of your entire plan and needs to accurately reflect what's in the body of the plan. It needs to match exactly.

Your Executive Summary should be short, simple, and organized in terms of the importance of the items highlighted here.

- Keep it short enough to give essential information but don't go into detail – that's what each section of the plan is for.
- Simplicity means using bullet points and subheadings. A good illustration or chart is effective here.
- It can be helpful to lead with why your business is needed and then list the factors to succeed in the marketplace by how relevant they are to that success.

Your Executive Summary paints a picture of your action plan. It whets the appetite of a potential financier to know more and to want to be involved. Many investors will screen opportunities based on what they read in the business plan. Make it relevant so they want to keep reading.

What should it include? Bplans.com offers this synopsis:

Who you are? Start with your business's name, location, and contact information.

What you offer and the problem your business solves. Include a brief description of the product or service you offer and why it's necessary. Your business doesn't need to serve a larger social problem, but it should address a need or opportunity in the market.

Your target markets. Sometimes the product itself defines the market, such as "Peoria's best Thai food," or "Mini Cooper dashboard accessory." If not, then a brief description of the target market.

Business plan purpose. Say whether you're seeking investment or trying to secure a bank loan. An executive summary is only necessary when you are sharing your business plan with outsiders.

<u>Size or scale</u>. For example, with an existing company, that information might be as simple as adding recent annual sales or number of employees to the basic company information in the first bullet here. For a startup, it might be a brief description of aspirations, such as a sales goal for the next year or three years from now. I often recommend a simple highlights chart, a bar chart with sales and gross margin for the next three years.

<u>Critical details</u>. Mention any defining details that would matter to the person that will ultimately read the summary–like that the founders are all MBA students at the local university, or that your business has been awarded a prestigious development grant. Remember, some readers will only look at the summary of your business plan.[v]

Again, you'll be pulling this information out of the body of your business plan. It's one of the easiest sections to write if you do it last.

From here on out don't be afraid to tell the full picture. Each section can be several pages. A thorough business plan, including financials and appendices can easily run 80 pages before supporting documentation. Don't worry if your plan gets long. The summary should be 3-5 pages, but the plan should be if it needs to be to give your potential financiers the information, they need to decide they want to work with you. A pizza parlor will need a smaller plan than a medical device inventor. The more complex your business, the more pages will be needed to properly convey the complexity, operating systems and financial picture.

This is another example of why it makes sense to answer these questions for yourself before writing them out for a reader. You may need to go through several drafts and reorganizations before you're comfortable with what you are presenting and how you are presenting it. You don't want to drown your potential investor in unnecessary prose or lists or details, but you absolutely want to present everything that's relevant. Don't be afraid of multiple drafts. You want a balance between thoroughness and succinctness.

Company Description

SmallBusiness.PatriotSoftware.com describes the business description as follows:

"A business description provides an overview of key aspects about your business, like what you do and what makes your business original. Anyone reading your company description should have no problem understanding the scope of your business idea."[vi]

As you start this section, be sure your goals and objectives are clear. TheBalanceCareers.com provides this example:

- An objective is to raise sales by 15%, reduce customer service costs by 8% and to increase product longevity by 22%.

- A goal is to be an industry leader in customer service or product standards.[vii]

Spell out your goals and objectives. Goals should be stated in the What and Why sections. Objectives should be spelled out in the How section, along with the systems that will achieve them.

Objectives are imperative to your business plan. How you will achieve your objectives needs to be outlined in this company description, the marketing plan, and the financial plan. They need to be interconnected and precise because they are interrelated in the operation of your business.

A basic company description involves the basic six questions of who, what where, when, why and how.

What – This describes your product or service. Are you a local pizza parlor? An online retailer? Describe what you are selling and what you expect top level revenues to be. Also discuss any product or service innovations, or other characteristics that make you unique in your marketplace or niche.

Where – Where are you located? Will you have business or industrial space? What are significant benefits of your geographical location? What is it about your location that is important to the success of your business?

When – When will you open for business? When will you see results? When will your important goals be reached, and what is the timing of your actions to achieve these goals? When will your lender be paid off or profits disbursed to investors?

Quick Tip: Don't forget to include an Exit Strategy here. Do you expect to retire from your business, sell it, or leave it to another generation to run? This is important because your exit strategy determines when your lender or investor gets paid off. It also gives context to growth and profit goals.

Why – Why will people or other businesses want to buy from you? What makes you different or gives you an advantage? How are you solving a problem that makes your business preferable to a competitor? Spell out the unique place you fill in your market that will drive customers to you.

This is a great place to add a mission statement.

How – How will your business be structure and why is that an optimum choice. Include any advisors you have – a business consultant, CPA, attorney, etc.- that will help you maintain this structure. How will you hire or terminate employees? How will you compensate them and what payroll system will you use? What are the actions steps that demonstrate how you will create a product or service, how you will sell it, and how you will turn a profit?

Quick Tip: Once you choose a company structure – LLC, 501(c)3 or C-Corporation – you won't be able to change it with a lender. They are investing in your company as it is structured at the time of the loan application. Investors may or may not have their own ideas about how you should be structure, and if you should change it before they invest.

This is also a great place to discuss your operating systems. Is there a specific software that helps you manage clients, track inventory or run payroll? Systems are what make a company run efficiently and effectively. You'll need to understand what systems you need, where to get software and machines, and how to implement the systems.

Don't skimp on this How section. This is the operational and action plan that you are promising to follow in order to pay off a loan or pay out to investors. If you don't properly convey the How, your investors won't trust that you know what you're doing.

While you don't need to include employee shifts, you do need to include key tasks that employees will complete. Do they need special certifications? Special uniforms or gear? Is your business seasonal and does that affects your workforce and inventory levels? These are the types of questions that need to be answered.

Quick Tip: Read any book on how to fix the problems in your target industry/business type. This will give you a solid understanding of what usually goes wrong, and how to both fix and prevent it from happening to you. Incorporate what you've learned as a system in your business. This shows investors you understand specific risks and are prepared for them.

If you really understand your business, you'll be able to describe it thoroughly and with precision. If you're having a hard time with it, you may need to step back and reflect on it. Just because the concept is clear in your head doesn't mean it's clear on paper. It must be clear.

Market Analysis

A Market Analysis is different than the Marketing Plan. Here you'll talk about the potential size of your customer pool and who your target customer is. The Market Analysis is "who" your customer is and how many you can reach. The Marketing Plan is "how" you will reach them.

A common misconception for most startups is confusing the entire market with the market you can reach. The entire market – the industry – may be $25.7 million people. But if you're a local business, you might only be reaching 15,000 people and you'll need them to be repeat customers.

In order to create an accurate analysis of the market you can reach, you need to understand how to define, locate and count potential customers. It is one of the more difficult sections to write, so be sure to take your time to learn and understand what it is and how you need to communicate it.

Now let's look at the elements you will need to include in your analysis.

Demographic Segmentation

Your ability to really define who your potential customers are, and to communicate it, will determine whether investors get the Why of your business. Your potential customer needs to seem real, with real preferences, real needs and real spending habits.

For consumer driven segmentation - define the characteristics of your potential customer like age, sex, gender, religion, education, income. You can also include elements like spending habits, brand preferences, education. Think of this to introduce your potential investor to your customer as if introducing colleagues.

For business to businesses companies, you'll discuss the size of the client company, total revenue, where they're located, how much on average they buy of your product or service a year, and other buying trends or innovation needs.

Showcase your understanding of who wants to do business with you. Craft your description here to fall in line with your What You Offer statement of the previous section. You can do this by describing your customer both numerically, as in the example below, as well as with narrative.

The narrative description of the company would discuss the differences between the big companies and small companies, and between the large and small companies in your target market. What is the need of the larger versus the smaller? What are the differences in buying trends? How fast they adopt new technology that dovetails with your offering? You'll need both to create a full picture for your investors.

The BusinessPlanShop.com has an infographic that sums it up.

There are two factors you need to look at when assessing the size of a market: the number of potential customers and the value of the market. It is very important to look at both numbers separately: let's take an example to understand why.

Imagine that you have the opportunity to open a shop either in Town A or in Town B.

Town	A	B
Market value	£200m	£100m
Potential customers	2 big companies	1,000 small companies
Competition	2 competitors	10 competitors

Table: Town A vs. Town B

Although Town B looks more competitive (10 competitors vs. 2 in Town A) and a smaller opportunity (market size of £100m vs. £200 in Town A), with 1,000 potential customers it is actually a more accessible market than Town A where you have only 2 potential customers.

viii

Target Market

This is how you subdivide your demographic data. A superhero movie appeals to 18-year-old boys, and a drama appeals to women over the age of 50. But the same movie company may make both films. If you were opening an ice cream shop, you would list how many families are in the area, and then break down the buying market by the frequency of teenagers, young families or grandparents are to purchase ice cream, ice cream cakes and related items.

Don't make this up or assume! Here is where a resource like the SBA.gov can make a big difference in the level of professional detail for your plan.

General business statistics	Find statistics on industries, business	NAICS, USA.gov Statistics, Statistical Abstract of the United States, U.S. Census

	conditions	Bureau
Consumer statistics	Gain info on potential customers, consumer markets	Consumer Credit Data, Consumer Product Safety
Demographics	Segment the population for targeting customers	American FactFinder, Bureau of Labor Statistics
Economic indicators	Know unemployment rates, loans granted and more	Consumer Price Index, Bureau of Economic Analysis
Employment statistics	Dig deeper into employment trends for your market	Employment and Unemployment Statistics
Income statistics	Pay your employees fair rates based on earnings data	Earnings by Occupation and Education, Income Statistics
Money and interest rates	Keep money by mastering exchange and interest rates	Daily Interest Rates, Money Statistics via Federal Reserve
Production and sales statistics	Understand demand, costs and consumer spending	Consumer Spending, Gross Domestic Product (GDP)
Trade statistics	Track indicators of sales and market performance	Balance of Payments, USA Trade Online
Statistics of specific industries	Use a wealth of federal agency data on industries	NAICS, Statistics of U.S. Businesses[ix]

Market Need/Demand

Is your business the thing that's missing in the neighborhood? Or the industry? Here is where you describe more about Why customers will choose your business. You'll need a thorough understanding of *what customers want*, not just what makes you different. This information needs to be referenced by research, data or a personal in-depth knowledge of the potential customers in your geographic or marketing reach. Aside from needing this information for your investors, you need it for YOU. If you don't truly understand what motivates your target market to buy your product or service, then you won't know how to market to them and convince them to shop with you.   The resources above can assist you in defining demand and trends.

Barriers to Entry

Another often misunderstood area, and easy to skip – but this is where you need to both understand and explain what the potential competition is. Maybe your competition already exists, but maybe it doesn't. If your offering is so good, what will prevent customers from coming in and stealing your customer base? Are there licenses, city fees, inspections, specialty equipment or training that makes it difficult to compete with you? Will competitors be able to retaliate with things like an established customer base in your niche or a larger advertising budget? Financiers need to know that you can create both a broad and deep customer base and protect it.

If you are entering a new market with high barriers to entry, will you be at a disadvantage that is difficult to overcome?   Do you have goals and objectives that will help you become a market leader and protect your expertise by building barriers? Learn.Mars.com explains it like this:

Barriers to entry are factors that prevent a startup from entering a market. They comprise one of the five forces that determine the intensity of competition in an industry (the others are industry rivalry, the bargaining power of buyers, the bargaining power of suppliers and the threat of substitutes). The intensity of competition in a certain field determines the attractiveness of a market (that is, low intensity means that the market is attractive).

Factors involved as barriers to entry may be either innocent (for example, the dominating company's absolute cost advantage) or deliberate (for example, high spending on advertising by incumbents makes it very expensive for new firms to enter the market).[x]

If you understand the barriers your business faces and have outlined how your objectives will successfully address them, then these barriers aren't necessarily a negative. In fact, your ability to make them work for your business will make your business more successful.

Regulations

As a follow up to Barriers to Entry, regulations are very important to address, even if you don't have many for your business. Financiers need to know that you understand exactly what the regulations are for your industry, and that you plan to comply with them in a way that makes your business better. The consequences of not knowing your industry's compliance issues are expensive. They may include fines, loss of revenues, lawsuits and even loss of the business. Let your potential investors know that you are prepared, and their money is safe with you.

If your business will be highly technical, involving things like Research and Development, then this section is an opportunity to show your expertise and shine. The more thoroughly you cover the regulations that will affect you, and discuss how you are going

Competition/Market Saturation

How do you figure out who your competition is and what that means for you? Here's where market segmentation can assist you. Once you understand who your customer is, you can better discuss the general competition for their dollars and choices.

Use Google or Yelp to find similar businesses that compete with you geographically. Read their reviews and visit their websites and social media profiles. How is your offering different? What sets the customer experience apart between your business and theirs? You can even visit their actual location.

Even if your competition is online, you can gain an understanding by how you plan to market. If you're going to use Social Media, do you know which of your competitors uses the same platforms? Do they advertise on YouTube or cable TV? Order something from them and see what their process is. Be resourceful and diligent.

Compare their strengths and weaknesses. What types of public relations and advertising do they employ as marketing strategies? Are their objectives defined, like focusing on a premium client – or maybe the low-hanging fruit?

How can you compete and reduce their market share? Will they respond or retaliate? What advantages will they have by being in the market before you? How can you make being new work to your advantage? Discuss why you're choosing to enter your chosen marketplace and define the elements that will affect your success.

TheBusinessPlanShop.com provides an excellent infographic to demonstrate how to show the size of the market and potential competition. Infographics like these are extremely helpful when illustrating comparative issues. It helps your investor understand the full picture of the market niche where you'll compete, who you're competing with, and what you're competing for.

Below is an example for a furniture shop in France. As you can see from the table all the actors on the market are currently focused on the low medium range of the market leaving the space free for a high end focused new player.

Company	Competitor 1 (Small shop)	Competitor 2 (Small shop)	Competitor 3 (Chain)	My Company
Revenues	€ 750,000	N.A.	€ 1,500,000	€ 400,000 (year 1 target)
Nb. employees	10	5	20	5
Size	1 shop in Caen, 1 shop in Cabourg	1 shop in Caen	3 shops in Caen	1 shop in Caen
Price	Low	Average	Average	High
Quality	Low	Average	Average	Superior
Choice	Large	Low	Very large	Average
Delivery	No	€ 50	Free from € 100	Free

Table: side by side competitive analysis

xi

Be realistic. It's not possible to be "the best" in each category. It's important to be the best choice in the categories that will get your target customers to buy from you or hire your service.

Organization and Management

This entire section is about structures – organization structures and team structures. This should be one of the easiest parts to write because this is usually very straightforward and the part most business owners know the most intimately.

Your Organization structure is simply the business structure – sole proprietorship, partnership, single or multi-member LLC, C-Corp or 501(c)3. Be sure to list the president and/or CEO, CFO and other key roles such as vice presidents and directors. SmartSheet.com provides this sample:

An *organizational chart* (also called an *organization chart*, and usually shortened to *org chart*) is a visual representation of the roles and reporting structure of a team, department, division, or an entire company.

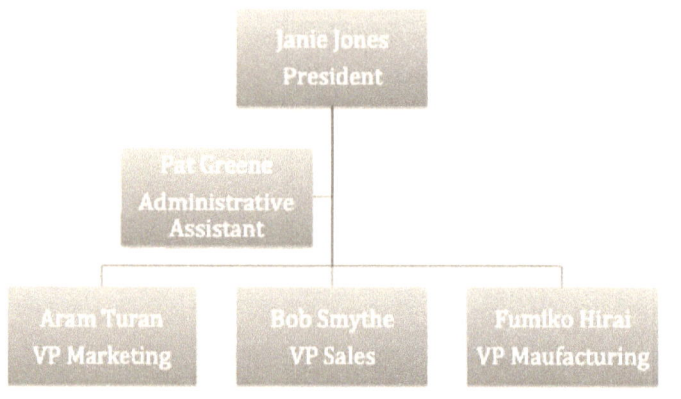

If you are a very small business and outsource work to contractors or freelancers, be sure to include outsourced work as part of the structure if their work is significant to your deliverables or operations.

Org Charts can be created in Microsoft products like Word or PowerPoint as well as in several number of business plan software packages. Clear is key here. It's also okay if you don't have all the key roles filled. Show the positions that you need to recruit and include that in your management team section below.

You Management Team should include all known owners and managers as well as potential key hires, support professionals and a board of directors if you have or will need one. You'll need to list all these players because your investors need to know who has authority to make decisions that will affect the success or failure of their business. Relevant experience is very important here, because inexperience means greater risk to the investment.

Quick Tip: Do not exaggerate. Do not list irrelevant details, recognitions or awards. Keep everything directly relevant and show that the qualifications of your people directly correlate to the success of goals and objectives.

Provide the following details for each key member of your team. This list from TheBalanceSMB.com is not exhaustive, but certainly provides a solid guideline:

- Name
- Percentage of ownership (LLC, corporation, etc.)
- Extent of involvement (active or silent partner)
- Type of ownership (stock options, general partner, etc.)
- Position in the business (CEO, CFO, etc.)
- Duties and responsibilities
- Educational background
- Experience or skills that are relevant to the business and the duties
- Past employment
- Skills will benefit the business
- Awards and recognition
- Compensation (how paid)
- How each persons' skills and experience will complement you and each other[xiii]

Here is where you want to give enough detail to create a picture of how each person will contribute to the success of your business, while not going into too much detail. The best way to do this is to describe the elements listed above that illustrates how the team member will directly affect goals, objectives and the bottom line.

If you have a Board of Directors, be sure to list their name, expertise and involvement with the company. If you don't have a Board of Directors but need one, list the positions and qualities you are looking to recruit.

You may not have a Board of Directors, but you still may have a Board of Advisors, or a team of people who advise you. These are often called Support Professionals. This may include lawyers, bankers, CPAs, and publicists as an example. Be sure to list these professionals with their titles, expertise, backgrounds and how they serve your business. Again, keep it relevant.

Service or Product

When you're excited about the product or service you'll be offering, this is a fun section to write. Describing your product or service should include the type of product, how it's used, and its value to the customer.

Start with the features of your product or service including things like size, speed, options or configurations. Be sure to focus on what sets you apart to your target market.

Discuss price – this includes the price to produce and the price you'll be charging. Be sure to tie the priced to the level of quality or usefulness to the consumer.

Does your product or service save time or money? How will you deliver it? Is it available all year round or is it seasonal or rare? How does that affect the price to produce or acquire it and then sell it?

If you've developed something that is cutting edge or new, this is a major competitive selling point. Discuss any patents, copyrights or trademarks you've applied for, costs of prototypes or testing and how soon you'll be bringing it to market.

Will your product or service require training for your customer or your employees? Do you need to provide some type of customer support? If you don't provide this in-house, do you have a way to provide it with a subcontractor or outside service partner?

Depending on the price of the product or service, will you be offering financing? Remember that financed payments count as revenue, but not cash flow until collected.

Think carefully about the level of Customer Service you'll need to provide. While that may mean an easy-to-use return policy for one business, it will be how staff interacts with clients for another. Now, Customer Service affects reputation, Yelp scores and your ability to charge a higher price for your products. Your customers should *want* to interact with you and feel comfortable doing so repeatedly. You'll want to outline your customer service policy and explain how it will create a positive customer experience.

Key knowledge, experience and endorsements should be discussed. This provides customers with a reason to trust you and a reason to refer their friends and family to you as well.

Delivery systems – How will your customers receive your product or service? Do you need a fleet of trucks or some very effective ice cream scoops and unique cones? Do you provide fast service, on-time service or trustworthy transportation? Maybe you package your product to make it easy for the customer to pick it up, install or use?

Inc.com lists some key questions to answer:
Are products or services in development or existing (and on the market)?
What is the timeline for bringing new products and services to market?

What makes your products or services different? Are there competitive advantages compared with offerings from other competitors? Are there competitive disadvantages you will need to overcome? (And if so, how?) Is price an issue? Will your operating costs be low enough to allow a reasonable profit margin?

How will you acquire your products? Are you the manufacturer? Do you assemble products using components provided by others? Do you purchase products from suppliers or wholesalers? If your business takes off, is a steady supply of products available?[xiv]

Don't forget other factors that might be unique to your business or industry. Entrepreneur Media offers this advice:

There are many wild cards unique to products, or perhaps simply little used industries, with which you can make your product stand out. For instance, consider a service agreement guarantee. When consumers know they can get a product repaired under a service guarantee or return a faulty product for a refund, they're often more likely to buy it over otherwise superior competitors offering less powerful warranties.[xv]

Be sure to include any future products or services you expect to offer within the next 5 years.

Marketing and Sales

Let's start by defining the difference between Marketing and Sales. Hubspot.com defines the difference as:

Sales and marketing are two business functions within an organization -- they both impact lead generation and revenue. The term, sales, refers to all activities that lead to the selling of goods and services. And marketing is the process of getting people interested in the goods and services being sold.[xvi]

Essentially - Marketing tells people you're selling something. Sales are when they buy/commit to pay you for a product or service.

Marketing

Your Marketing section will explain how you're going to tell people they can buy from you. But this means you first need to know where they're looking for you. Do your customers find their information on businesses like yours on social media or print advertising? Do they check with the Better Business Bureau or Yelp for reviews? Will a coupon offer get people to try your service, or do you need to send a salesperson to their office for a presentation? How do your competitors reach their customers?

Quick Tip: Part of understanding good marketing is knowing what *not* to do. This could mean that your offer is better received as a postcard in the mailbox than an ad on cable TV. It could also mean that you should put more money into advertising on Pinterest than on Facebook. The better you understand this, the more targeted and effective your marketing dollars will be.

The more you know your industry, your target market and your niche, the better you'll be at choosing which marketing vehicles work best for your venture.

- Advertising – in magazines, on billboard, on radio or TV, Google AdWords or direct mail
- Social Media strategies and posts – Facebook, Twitter, Instagram, LinkedIn, Pinterest
- A Website – a must in today's marketplace
- Establish a network – this can be achieved by joining chambers or business associations, sponsoring a sports team, and participating in networking events.

- Press and publicity – throw a newsworthy event or donate to a charity to get the press to cover you. Keep in mind that hiring a professional publicist will often give you an edge on your competition.
- Create special offers – ideally something that can be easily shared physically or online by customers

The most important key to marketing is to create a long-term plan, budget for it, keep your expectations realistic, and repeat, repeat, repeat. Forbes.com says it well here:

If you build it, they still may not come. You must get out there and tell people who you are, why your product or service is different from the competition and how to find you. Advertising is not a one-size fits all solution. Find what works for you, but whatever you do, you must advertise.

More than anything, focus on consistent, repetitive branding. Many marketing professionals believe in the "rule of seven," which means people need to hear or see your message at least seven times before taking any action. In today's world of constant connectivity, you must make sure you're seen and heard. The most common reason that people do not buy your product is that they do not know about it yet.[xvii]

A good marketing plan is detailed but it also includes resources that make it top-notch. If you can't hire an actual marketing company, or don't have an in-house marketing team, you can find freelance professionals and resources at sites like CreativeMarket.com, Fiverr.com, and UpWork.com. You can hire freelancers to create graphics, write content, design logos, or even write your plan for you.

Do you need beautiful photos to help dress up your plan, but you can't afford a photo shoot? Try online sites that offer license-free images like Unsplash.com or Pixabay.com. Pixabay even offers license-free video clips you can use to design ads, promotions, or even a company video.

Maybe you know you need a Social Media strategy, but you don't know how to create one that gets results. Try one of the big two companies that offer tutorials and systems:

Hootsuite.com – For a monthly fee, Hootsuite will help you schedule your posts, manage your content and track your results. They also have a library of videos that will train you in all aspects of social media, SEO, and online advertising. You can hire freelance professionals who are certified through Hootsuite to help as well.[xviii]

Hubspot.com – This free service is a Customer Retention Management (CRM) system that will help you track sales and better understand your customer. The goal is to help you grow through lead generation, marketing automation, analytics, email tracking, and customer feedback management. They also offer free videos that cover marketing, sales, advertising, social media promotions and SEO training. [xix]

During writing your marketing plan, don't forget about branding. Branding is more than a logo design and color package. Branding is about creating a message that resonates with how your clients see themselves, and how you fit into that image. In her book, "Fascinate – How to Make Your Brand Impossible to Resist," Sally Hogshead writes:

"Often, when people *buy* a product, they are actually *paying* for an intangible benefit. When buying Chanel sunglasses, women are paying for the logo… This is the heart of differentiation. It's tough to be better. But far easier to be different…You're crafting messages that people want. Instead of barging in on tightly protected attention spans, you're enticing the right people to become more deeply involved with you."[xx]

If your business is a pharmacy, your customers value trust and accuracy. Your marketing messages will need to use words and images that convey you are trustworthy and accurate. If you are selling pizza, your customers probably value quality and community – so your message will convey the service experience of being with family at your restaurant and the satisfying taste of your product. Your pharmacy shouldn't look like a dining environment and your pizza parlor shouldn't look sterile.

Including even a small paragraph or two about the brand of your enterprise and how you will convey it tells potential investors that you are inviting your customers into a relationship with you, not merely begging them to buy from you. Not only will it help you entice customers, you'll entice investors as well.

Sales

Don't forget to talk about how you will sell your product or service. Will customers pay cash or use credit at the time of purchase? Will you use receipts, contracts or invoices? If using contracts or invoices, what are the payment terms? Be sure to explain how revenue will convert into cash flow, and when.

Will customers carry the product out of your shop, or will it be delivered? Is it a local delivery with your own dedicated vehicle, or will you use a service like USPS, FedEx or UPS? Will your services be provided by professionals, staff, technicians or the internet? How will you measure customer satisfaction? How will you handle returns or disputes?

If your sales process has multiple steps, include a diagram or infographic. Sales chain illustrations provide clarity. A good picture really is worth a thousand words – especially because at this point in the business plan most financiers appreciate less reading. That doesn't mean you can skip the descriptions. Use the two together to create a mental picture that delivers an accurate image of how you will make money.

The complexity of what you sell and how you sell it will determine the length of this section. The objective here is to clarify what it will take to exchange a product or service for money.

Funding Request

You've gone to all this effort to write a good business plan. If you're going to give it to a potential investor for review, you don't want to forget to ask for money. There are a few key points to include, which IntrepidExecutiveGroup.com shares:

A funding request is exactly what it sounds like: a written request to obtain funding from a lender or investor for your business. It's typically included as part of the overall business plan, specifically focusing on the business's funding needs. Whether you're seeking capital from a traditional bank, private investor, or angel investor, you should create a funding request. It's a critical element that increases your chance of getting approved for funding.[xxi]

How much money do you need right now? This is the *current* need to operate your business. You can calculate this by counting all your operating costs against revenue. If you're going to need operating funds for several years, add that here as well. Often potential investors prefer which stage of growth they want to fund. Some will take entry-level risks. Others want some demonstrated capacity to do what you say and get the results you promise. Still others like to capital major expansions after a business has hit earlier milestones. If you can secure financing up front, go for it! But be aware that capital for long-term payoffs often require multiple stages of investment funds.

Quick Tip: Specify if your funding request is for equity or debt financing. It's a simple detail, but an obvious one you don't want to overlook.

Elements to include in this section start with telling potential financiers how the funding will be used at each stage. This includes capital expenditures, acquisitions, payroll, merchandise/stock, machinery, employee training, special certifications, etc.

Create a timeline for funding needs, expenses, revenue generation and payoff. If your request is for stages of growth, make sure your timeline illustrates that. Your lender or investor needs to know when you need the funds, and when it will be recouped. Use a graphic if the timeline covers multiple years or complex stages.

Financial Projections

This is your most important section. Even though your financial projections are only estimating, what matters is how you calculate and present those estimates. Your financial savvy will show here – for better or for worse.

Avoid overly optimistic or overly pessimistic scenarios. Show realism – it's rare that sales are flat for months then suddenly shoot up in a straight line like a hockey stick[xxii]. Changes should relate to your marketing timeline and seasonal sales cycles, and your ability to show an interrelated pattern of exposure and sales growth will show you understand how marketing influences sales. A credible business plan demonstrates realism. And while you might not write the financial projects sequentially, you should present them that way.

Tim Berry, president and founder of Palo Alto Software and blogger at Bplans.com say this:

> "It's not tax reporting. It's an elaborate educated guess."[xxiii]

Projected Sales Forecast

Begin by projecting your sales over a period of 1 and 3 years for less complex business, and up to 5 or 10 into the future if your business involves research or complex product cycles and long-term payment contracts.   You'll want to make some estimate of sales over the life of the loan, or long enough for investors to see their returns.

Using a program like Excel, you can create a spreadsheet that calculates the units you hope to sell, their costs, their sales price, the margin (price – costs), and how many units you expect to sell monthly and annually.   If you have a new business, make an educated guess based on what you think the results of your marketing will be.   New businesses also have slowed up front sales.   If you've budgeted for a special event, a promotional campaign, or a lot of social media advertising, the timing of these events should be reflected in your sales projects.

Projected Expense Budget

When creating expenses, be sure to address the difference between fixed costs, variable costs and overhead costs.

- Fixed costs are things like the machines that produce the product.
- Variable costs are the materials that go into each unit.
- Overhead costs are the expenses for your support staff, seasonal workers, etc.

Know the difference and be able to discuss them and show them numerically.

Always account for how growth in sales affects these costs.   Unit costs usually drop when you buy in greater bulk, but fixed costs and asset investments go up because you need more machines to make the unit. Even in-service businesses, if your sales increase, so does your sales force, your HR department, and your customer service department.

Projected Cash Flow Statement

Remember that revenue and cash flow are different. A cash flow statement only shows when cash comes into the business. If you use invoicing and contracts, you'll need to show the lag time for when payments are made.

There are software systems for business planning and projections that can be very useful here. But you don't want to be caught off guard by underestimating your expense cycle and underestimating your cash. Aside from telling investors you have unrealistic expectations, it can destroy your business.

Projected Income Projection

Your Pro-Forma Income Statement will detail profits and losses over the forecasted period. These are benchmarks for budgeting and operational considerations throughout your forecast period.

$$Sales - Cost\ of\ Sales = Gross\ Margin$$
$$Gross\ Margin - (Expenses + Interest + Taxes) = Net\ Profit$$

Use the numbers from your previous three sections – Projected Sales, Projected Expenses and Projected Cash Flow to create these documents. Corporate Financial Institute presents a simple diagram that shows what a pro forma income statement should look like.

	Income Statement Template	2014	2015	2016	2017	2018
						This file is for educational purposes only. E&OE
	Revenue	102,007	118,086	131,345	142,341	150,772
	Cost of Goods Sold (COGS)	39,023	48,004	49,123	52,654	56,710
	Gross Profit	62,984	70,082	82,222	89,687	94,062
	Expenses					
	Salaries and Benefits	26,427	22,058	23,872	23,002	25,245
	Rent and Overhead	10,963	10,125	10,087	11,020	11,412
	Depreciation & Amortization	19,500	18,150	17,205	16,544	16,080
	Interest	2,500	2,500	1,500	1,500	1,500
	Other	8,820	6,225	1,659	3,911	5,996
	Total Expenses	68,210	59,658	54,323	55,977	60,233
	Earnings Before Tax	(5,226)	10,424	27,899	33,711	33,829
	Taxes	1,120	4,858	8,481	10,908	11,598
	Net Earnings	(6,346)	5,566	19,416	22,802	22,231

CFI

Corporate Finance Institute®
https://corporatefinanceinstitute.org/

xxiv

Yours will be more thorough and reflect the specifics of your business. If you've used only Excel up to this point, you'll need to find a software program if you're not familiar with how to calculate this manually. This is a good time to bring in some expert help, especially since your fundability depends on it.

Quick Tip: There is a difference between an unprofessional financial statement and a rudimentary one. If you know your numbers and can support them, simple is good. But the more complex your business, the more you need professional looking statements.

Projected Balance Sheet

A pro-forma balance sheet is where you show assets and liabilities. Inc.com quotes Tim Berry again:

You must deal with assets and liabilities that aren't in the profits and loss statement and project the net worth of your business at the end of the fiscal year. Some of those are obvious and affect you at only the beginning, like startup assets. A lot are not obvious. "Interest is in the profit and loss, but repayment of principle isn't," Berry says. "Taking out a loan, giving out a loan, and inventory show up only in assets--until you pay for them." So, the way to compile this is to start with assets, and estimate what you'll have on hand, month by month for cash, accounts receivable (money owed to you), inventory if you have it, and substantial assets like land, buildings, and equipment. Then figure out what you have as liabilities--meaning debts. That's money you owe because you haven't paid bills (which is called accounts payable) and the debts you have because of outstanding loans.[xxv]

Assets and Liabilities aren't sales and expenses. Assets are fixtures like machines and office furniture. Cash is an asset. Liabilities are debts. An expense is a bill or a payment. A liability is the balance of the debt minus payments to date.

Balance sheets can be tricky because most business people think in terms of money, not value. The value of a company's assets must equal the value of liabilities and equity. Don't hesitate to hire a CPA or qualified professional to help you get this right.

Projected Break-Even Analysis

Your break-even point (BEP) is when your sales and/or service volume match your expenses. This is the point where Sales – Expenses = Zero.

Colleen Egan, author of "Break-Even Analysis 101: How to Calculate BEP and Apply It to Your Business" writes:

To calculate a break-even point based on units: Divide fixed costs by the revenue per unit minus the variable cost per unit. The fixed costs are those that do not change no matter how many units are sold. The revenue is the price for which you're selling the product minus the variable costs, like labor and materials.

Break-Even Point (Units) =
Fixed Costs ÷ (Revenue per Unit – Variable Cost per Unit)

When determining a break-even point based on sales dollars: Divide the fixed costs by the contribution margin. The contribution margin is determined by subtracting the variable costs from the price of a product. This amount is then used to cover the fixed costs.

Break-Even Point (sales dollars) = Fixed Costs ÷ Contribution Margin

Contribution Margin = Price of Product – Variable Costs[xxvi]

Why is this important? Because you need to know the point in your business life cycle where your expenses are covered by sales, so that you know when you start generating actual profit.

What you will present in this financial section is the summary data by month/quarters and years. The supporting spreadsheets with data and calculations will go in the appendix.

There's no need to panic if this creating financial reports isn't your strength. You just need to demonstrate a pragmatic understanding of how to make money. You also need to understand the difference between a lender, an angel investor and a venture capitalist. You'll want to write to the proper intended audience.

Quick Tip: Use visuals. If you need help with these, use a freelancer to create some for you.

Appendix

The body of the business plan is for your top points and summaries. Yes, there's detail, but most of the truly detailed documentation goes into your appendix. US.Accion.Org provides a list to help:

- Credit histories for both the business and its owners
- Business and personal tax returns

- Resumes of the owners and key management
- Photos of your products or their prototypes
- Samples of marketing materials, logos, and mockup ads
- Reference letters from business associates and community leaders
- Details of your market research studies
- Information about your competitors
- Press clippings about you and the business
- Any relevant news articles on your product or industry
- Legal documents such as your incorporation papers, shareholder certificates, etc.
- Copies of patents, permits or licenses you hold
- Copies of your property and equipment leases or rental agreements
- Contact info for your professional staff, including your accountant and attorney
- Contracts for current or future work
- Spreadsheets and documentation for financial projections[xxvii]

Keep the documents organized in the same order they refer to the body of the plan. You can number them which makes it easier to refer to them in previous section, such as "Please refer to Appendix Item 11" or a similar organization structure. Be just as meticulous preparing the appendix as you did in previous sections.

3. SUMMARY

As with every other section of this business plan, how you describe your business as an operating venture will serve you as well as explain your venture to your investors. The clearer you are about how to make your business work – the clearer your investors will be about why they should invest in you or underwrite your loan.

Just as importantly, the more realistic your business plan as an operating guide, the more likely you are to hit your goals and objectives. Some lenders and investors consider it a breach of contract if you write one thing but do another. You can be sued and lose everything. So be honest. Be realistic. Be trustworthy.

By doing the necessary prep work and home work – learning what you don't know, getting advice and help, and being honest with yourself about what it will take for this venture to be successful, you'll also sleep better knowing you're taking a good risk yourself.

4. REFERENCES

i "What Percentage of Small Business Fail," by Georgia McIntyre, September 10, 2019

ii "Why startups fail, according to their founders." By Erin Griffith, September 25, 2014. https://fortune.com/2014/09/25/why-startups-fail-according-to-their-founders/

iii "The Unexpected Connection: Credit Scores and Your Business Plan," by Sherry Gray, April 7, 2016. https://www.business.com/articles/credit-scores-and-your-business-plan/

iv "Revenue vs Profit vs. Cash Flow' Know the Danger" by Blaine Bertsch, April 14, 2019. https://dryrun.com/revenue-vs-profit-vs-cash-flow/

v "How to Write an Executive Summary" by Tim Berry, 2019 https://articles.bplans.com/writing-an-executive-summary/

vi "How to Write a Company Description for a Business Plan" by Rachel Blakely-Gray, December 9, 2016 https://smallbusiness.patriotsoftware.com/how-to-write-company-description-business-plan/

vii "Overview of a General Business Plan Company Description" by Lahle Wolfe, October 22, 2019 https://www.thebalancecareers.com/write-great-business-plan-4021217

viii "How to do a market analysis for a business plan," TheBusinessPlanShop.com https://www.thebusinessplanshop.com/blog/en/entry/market_analysis_for_business_plan

ix "Market research and competitive analysist" at SBA.gov https://www.sba.gov/business-guide/plan-your-business/market-research-competitive-analysis x "Barriers to entry: Factors preventing startups from entering a market," at Learn.Mars.com https://learn.marsdd.com/article/barriers-to-entry-factors-preventing-startups-from-entering-a-market/

xi "How to do a market analysis for a business plan," TheBusinessPlanShop.com https://www.thebusinessplanshop.com/blog/en/entry/market_analysis_for_business_plan

xii "How to Easily Create an Organization Chart in Word" at SmartSheet.com https://www.smartsheet.com/easy-org-charts-in-word

xiii "How to Write Organization and Management Section of Your Biz Plan" by Randy Duermyer, September 30, 2019 https://www.thebalancesmb.com/business-plan-organization-and-management-section-1794228

xiv "How to Write a Great Business Plan: Products and Services," by Jeff Haden, April 6, 2015 https://www.inc.com/jeff-haden/how-to-write-a-great-business-plan-products-and-services.html

xv "How to Excite Readers with Your Business Plan's Product Section. (Yes, Seriously.) by The Staff of Entrepreneur Media, Inc. December 18, 2014 https://www.entrepreneur.com/article/239410

xvi "What's the Difference Between Sales and Marketing? A Simple & Easy Primer" by Meredith Hart, February 21, 2019 https://blog.hubspot.com/sales/sales-and-marketing

xvii "Small Business Marketing 101" by Elizabeth Pritchett, January 23, 2018 https://www.forbes.com/sites/forbesbusinessdevelopmentcouncil/2018/01/23/small-business-marketing-101/#4e05445c45ff

xviii https://hootsuite.com/

xix https://www.hubspot.com/

xx "Fascinate – How to Make Your Brand Impossible to Resist," by Sally Hogshead, HarperCollins Books, copyright 2010, pp 24, 25 and 27.

[xxi] "How to Create a Funding Request" by Intrepid Capital Group, March 2, 2017 https://www.intrepidexecutivegroup.com/blog/create-funding-request/

[xxii] "How to Write the Financial Section of a Business Plan" by Elizabeth Wasserman https://www.inc.com/guides/business-plan-financial-section.html

[xxiii] "How to Write the Financial Section of a Business Plan" by Elizabeth Wasserman https://www.inc.com/guides/business-plan-financial-section.html

[xxiv] "Income Statement Definition Explanation and Examples Sample Balance Sheet" https://golagoon.com/balance-sheet-and-income-statement-template/income-statement-definition-explanation-and-examples-sample-balance-sheet-xls-template-dow/

[xxv] "How to Write the Financial Section of a Business Plan" by Elizabeth Wasserman https://www.inc.com/guides/business-plan-financial-section.html

[xxvi] "Break Even Analysis 101: How to Calculate BEP and Apply It to Your Business" by Colleen Egan, https://squareup.com/us/en/townsquare/how-to-calculate-break-even-point-analysis

[xxvii] "Business Plan Section 9: Appendix" https://us.accion.org/resource/business-plan-section-9-appendix/